From Exploration to Fulfillment: Find Your Life Purpose and Live in Harmony with It

Book Summary:

The book "From Exploration to Fulfillment: Find Your Life Purpose and Live in Harmony with It" provides a practical guide to help readers discover their life purpose and live it meaningfully. Through a combination of self-exploration, purpose identification, and action planning, readers will be able to overcome obstacles and create a life aligned with their true purpose. The ultimate goal is to help readers live in harmony with their purpose, experiencing gratitude, happiness, and personal fulfillment.

Introduction:

The Importance of Finding Your Life Purpose and Living in Harmony with It

Chapter 1: The Importance of Having a Life Purpose

- Explore the meaning and significance of having a life purpose
- The benefits of living in harmony with one's purpose

Chapter 2: Self-Exploration

- Recognize your unique passions, values, and talents
- Work on self-awareness and self-knowledge
- Explore significant life experiences that have shaped your identity

Chapter 3: Identifying Your Life Purpose

- Utilize practical tools to identify your life purpose

- Explore different areas of life (personal, professional, relationships) in relation to your purpose

- Strengthen the connection between personal passions and impact on the world

Chapter 4: Overcoming Obstacles

- Address fears and resistances that may hinder the journey towards your purpose

- Develop strategies to manage self-sabotage and negativity

- Embrace failures as opportunities for growth and learning

Chapter 5: Creating an Action Plan

- Define clear and measurable goals aligned with your life purpose

- Develop an action plan to achieve your purpose step by step

- Maintain motivation and commitment along the way

Chapter 6: Living in Harmony with Your Purpose

- Integrate your life purpose into all aspects of daily life

- Experience gratitude, happiness, and fulfillment through connection with your purpose

- Create a balanced and fulfilling life that aligns with your purpose

Conclusion:

Final reflections on the journey towards your life purpose and the importance of living in harmony with it Appendix: Practical exercises, guiding questions, and additional resources to support readers in their journey towards discovering their life purpose.

Introduction

Welcome to my ebook, "From Exploration to Fulfillment: Find Your Life Purpose and Live in Harmony with It." These pages are dedicated to those who seek to give deep and lasting meaning to their existence by discovering their life purpose and living in full harmony with it.

The search for our life purpose is a personal journey of inner exploration, reflection, and authenticity. When we have a clear life purpose, we feel inspired, motivated, and guided in our personal growth and fulfillment. Our purpose provides an internal compass, guiding us towards choices and actions that resonate with our true essence.

This ebook has been created to assist you on this personal journey of discovery. We will explore the importance of finding your life purpose and how to live in harmony with it. You will discover that your purpose is not something external to you but rather something that resides within you, unique and unparalleled.

Through a combination of reflections, practical exercises, and effective tools, I will guide you through the process of discovering your life purpose. We will delve into your passions, values, talents, and the experiences that have shaped your identity. I will support you in overcoming internal obstacles such as fear and self-sabotage that may hinder your path to realizing your purpose.

Once you have identified your life purpose, I will guide you in creating a concrete action plan to fully live it. You will learn how to integrate your purpose into every aspect of your life, from personal relationships to your professional career. I encourage you to cultivate a mindset of gratitude, trust, and resilience that will sustain you along the journey.

No matter where you are in your journey, this ebook will provide you with a roadmap to find your life purpose and live in harmony with it. I hope you embrace your authenticity, discover your limitless potential, and create a meaningful and fulfilling life. Get ready to

embark on a journey of self-realization
because your search for life purpose begins
here and now.

Chapter 1:
The Importance of
Having a Life Purpose

Life is an extraordinary journey, a unique opportunity to explore, grow, and discover our true potential. In this journey, we often find ourselves questioning the meaning and importance of our existence. There are moments when we feel lost, without a clear direction or a goal to aspire to. That is why understanding the importance of having a life purpose becomes crucial. In this chapter, we will explore the profound meaning of a purpose and the benefits that come from living in harmony with it.

Exploring the Meaning and Importance of Having a Life Purpose:

A life purpose can be defined as the inner force that guides us, giving us a sense of direction and meaning in life. It is what propels us out of bed in the morning with passion and determination. A purpose can take various forms: it could be a specific goal to achieve, an activity that deeply impassions us, or even a lasting imprint we want to leave on the world. Regardless of its form, a life purpose offers us a sense of meaning and connection to something greater than ourselves.

The Significance of Having a Life Purpose:

Having a life purpose is fundamental to our well-being and personal fulfillment. When we live without a clear purpose, we often feel lost, confused, and lacking direction. The absence of a purpose can lead to a sense of inner emptiness and a loss of motivation. On the contrary, having a clear life purpose gives us a sense of meaning and belonging to the world. It gives us a reason to wake up in the morning with enthusiasm and determination, driving us to overcome obstacles along the way.

A life purpose helps us make sense of our actions and choices. It allows us to look beyond the small daily challenges and focus on something bigger and more elevated. When we have a purpose, our actions acquire a deeper meaning, and we feel part of something greater than ourselves. This sense of connection grants us lasting joy and a sense of fulfillment.

The Benefits of Living in Harmony with Your Purpose:

Living in harmony with our life purpose allows us to experience profound personal fulfillment. We feel aligned with our true essence and live an authentic life. When we live our purpose, we engage our skills and passions, bringing forth our highest potential. This personal fulfillment brings about lasting inner satisfaction, regardless of external circumstances. We feel content and at peace with ourselves because we are living in accordance with who we truly are.

Having a well-defined life purpose provides us with a sense of direction and orientation in life. We know which values are important to us and what goals we want to pursue. This clarity helps us make decisions in line with our purpose, avoiding the dispersion of energy and resources in activities that do not propel us forward. When we have a purpose, we can focus our energies on what truly matters and create a meaningful path towards our life purpose. This provides us with an internal guide that allows us to make conscious choices and live a life aligned with what we consider important.

Living in harmony with our life purpose grants us the inner strength necessary to face and overcome the challenges we encounter along the way. When we are aware of our purpose, we are more motivated to persevere, even when things get difficult. Challenges become opportunities for growth and learning, and our determination pushes us to find creative solutions and surpass obstacles that might otherwise discourage us. When we have an inspiring purpose, we are willing to step out of our comfort zone and confront challenges with courage and determination. Resilience becomes part of our life journey, and we are able to transform adversity into opportunities for personal growth.

Conclusion:

In this chapter, we have explored the profound meaning of a life purpose and the benefits that come from living in harmony with it. Having a purpose grants us a sense of meaning and direction, fueling our personal fulfillment and inner satisfaction. It provides us with an internal compass that guides us in life and gives us the strength to overcome the challenges we encounter along the way. Now that we have understood the importance of having a life purpose, we can embark on the journey to discover our own and live it fully. It is through our purpose that we can find true happiness, fulfillment, and leave a significant imprint on the world.

Chapter 2:
Self-Exploration

In the journey towards a meaningful and fulfilling life, it is essential to embark on a journey of self-exploration. Self-exploration allows us to discover our passions, values, and unique talents, as well as deepen self-awareness and self-knowledge. In this chapter, we will explore the processes of self-exploration and how they can help us better understand who we are and how we have been shaped by significant life experiences.

Recognizing Your Passions, Values, and Unique Talents:

Passions are activities or interests that deeply excite us and make us feel alive. Recognizing our passions requires an open mind and a willingness to explore different activities. We can observe what truly excites us, the activities that make us lose track of time, and those that give us a sense of fulfillment. Identifying our passions allows us to align our actions with what brings us joy and satisfaction.

Values are guiding principles that help us make decisions, determine what we consider important in life, and influence our actions. Identifying our values requires deep reflection on what we deem fundamental and meaningful. We can examine which qualities or ideals resonate with us and guide our choices. Defining our values provides us with an internal compass to live in alignment with what we consider most precious.

Each of us has unique talents and abilities that can be developed and used for our own benefit and for the surrounding world. Recognizing our talents requires self-reflection and attention to activities in which we excel and that give us a sense of fulfillment. Harnessing our talents enables us to give our best, achieve extraordinary results, and make a significant contribution in our areas of giftedness.

Working on Self-Awareness and Self-Knowledge:

Self-awareness is the ability to observe and understand our thoughts, emotions, and behaviors. Cultivating self-awareness requires a practice of non-judgmental self-observation. We can dedicate time to reflection, meditation, or techniques like journaling to explore our thoughts and feelings. Self-awareness allows us to develop a deeper understanding of ourselves and the patterns that drive our actions.

Self-knowledge is the process of acquiring a thorough understanding of oneself, including aspects such as preferences, fears, weaknesses, and strengths. We can explore self-knowledge through reflection, actively listening to our thoughts and feelings, and even through feedback from others. Self-knowledge enables us to accept our imperfections and work on them, as well as value and develop our strengths.

Exploring Significant Life Experiences That Have Shaped Our Identity:

The life experiences we have faced play a fundamental role in shaping our identity. We can reflect on the significant experiences we have lived, both positive and negative, and seek to extract lessons from them. We can consider how these experiences have influenced our beliefs, values, and aspirations. Through reflection on these experiences, we can gain a deeper understanding of ourselves

and the factors that have made us who we
are today.

The challenges we have encountered in life
can be transformed into opportunities for
personal growth. We can examine the
difficulties we have overcome and consider
how they have made us stronger, more
resilient, and wiser. These experiences teach
us to overcome obstacles, develop self-
confidence, and cultivate a mindset of
continuous learning. By exploring the
challenges we have overcome, we can find a
sense of gratitude for our experiences and
greater confidence in our ability to face future
adversities.

Conclusion:

In this chapter, we have explored the process of self-exploration and how we can recognize our passions, values, and unique talents. We have also delved into the importance of self-awareness and self-knowledge in the journey of self-exploration. Lastly, we have explored how significant life experiences can shape our identity and how we can transform challenges into opportunities for personal growth. Through self-exploration, we can gain a deeper understanding of ourselves, live in alignment with what excites us, and develop greater awareness of how our experiences have shaped us.

Chapter 3:
Discovering Your Life Purpose

Discovering your life purpose is a venture that requires deep exploration and introspection. In this chapter, we will focus on using practical tools to identify your life purpose. We will also explore the different spheres of life, such as personal, professional, and relationships, and how they relate to our purpose. Finally, we will examine how to strengthen the connection between our personal passions and the impact we desire to make in the world.

Using practical tools to identify your life purpose:

Values are guiding principles that indicate what we consider important in life. To identify your life purpose, it is essential to explore your core values. You can use tools such as values reflection exercises or creating a list of your most significant values. These tools help you understand which principles are at the core of your existence and define the direction you want to take in life.

Each of us possesses unique abilities and talents. Identifying and harnessing these qualities can provide valuable clues to discovering your life purpose. Reflect on activities that deeply resonate with you and where you excel, considering how you can utilize these skills to make a difference. Seek feedback from friends and family to recognize your strengths and distinctive abilities.

Significant life experiences can offer valuable insights into understanding your life purpose. Reflect on experiences that have excited you, taught you something important, or had a significant impact on your worldview. Examining these experiences may reveal common themes or recurring values that can guide you in defining your purpose.

Exploring the different spheres of life in relation to your purpose:

The personal sphere concerns your well-being and individual fulfillment. Exploring your life purpose in this sphere requires deep reflection on your personal aspirations, growth goals, and activities that bring you joy and satisfaction. Ask yourself what makes you feel most alive and grateful, and consider how you can integrate these experiences into your daily life.

The professional sphere pertains to work and career. Exploring your life purpose in this sphere involves seeking work that aligns with your values, passions, and skills. Examine how your work can contribute to something greater than yourself and how you can leverage your abilities to make a difference in the world through your profession.

The sphere of relationships involves your connections with others, such as family, friends, partners, and community. Exploring your life purpose in this sphere means considering how you can have a positive impact on the lives of the people around you. Ask yourself how you can cultivate meaningful relationships, provide support, and inspire others through your actions and values.

Strengthening the connection between personal passions and impact on the world:

Personal passions are what deeply excite and fulfill us. To strengthen the connection between our passions and the impact on the world, it is important to clearly and specifically identify our passions. Explore activities that ignite your enthusiasm, make you feel "in the flow," and fill you with positive energy. These passions can indicate the type of impact you desire to have in the world.

Once you have identified your personal passions, reflect on the impact you want to have on the world. Ask yourself what kind of change or improvement you want to bring to people's lives or the environment around you. Defining the desired impact helps provide a clear direction for your life purpose and focuses your actions toward a meaningful goal.

Once your passions and desired impact are identified, it is important to translate them into concrete actions. Seek opportunities that allow you to put your passions into practice and make a difference in the world. These actions can be small or large, depending on your capabilities and resources, but what matters is that they align with your purpose and bring you closer to achieving the desired impact.

Conclusion:

In this chapter, we have explored the use of practical tools to identify your life purpose. We have also examined how to explore the different spheres of life in relation to your purpose, such as the personal, professional, and relationships spheres. Lastly, we have addressed the importance of strengthening the connection between our personal passions and the impact we desire to have on the world. By continuing on this journey of discovering your life purpose, you will be able to align your actions with what truly excites you and contribute significantly to your own well-being and that of others.

Chapter 4:

Overcoming Obstacles

Facing Fears and Resistance that Can Hinder the Path to Your Purpose:

Fears and resistance can act as powerful barriers that prevent us from getting closer to our life purpose. These negative emotions can manifest in different ways, such as the fear of failure, the fear of judgment from others, the fear of change, or the fear of stepping out of our comfort zone. Confronting these fears requires courage and self-awareness.

To address fears, it is crucial to identify and understand their underlying reasons. Ask yourself what scares you and why. Often, fears result from limiting beliefs or past negative experiences. Explore these beliefs and challenge them with positive thoughts and actions. Remember that fears are often irrational and not based on reality, and overcoming them can open up new opportunities and possibilities for growth.

Resistance is another common obstacle that can manifest as self-sabotage or procrastination. It can be the internal voice telling you that you're not good enough or that it's not worth trying. To overcome resistance, you need to identify and understand its roots. Ask yourself what is holding you back and what thoughts or behavior patterns are limiting your progress. Confront resistance with determination and commitment, focusing on the actions you can take to overcome it.

Developing Strategies to Manage Self-Sabotage and Negativity:

Self-sabotage is a destructive behavior that undermines our efforts in pursuing our life purpose. It can manifest through self-criticism and self-judgment, leading us to procrastinate or give up on our goals. To manage self-sabotage, it is important to cultivate self-compassion and self-esteem.

Practice self-compassion to accept your flaws and imperfections. Recognize that failure is part of the learning process and that it is normal to make mistakes along the way. Treat yourself with kindness and support, as you would do for a friend facing a challenge.

Maintain a positive perspective and focus on your strengths and the successes you have achieved.

Negativity is another limiting force that can undermine our path to success. It can come from external influences, such as criticism from others, but it can also originate internally through the critical voice in our mind. To manage negativity, practice positive thinking and gratitude.

Cultivate a positive mindset, focusing on the positive aspects of your life and the progress you have made. Recognize and celebrate even the smallest successes. Be grateful for the opportunities that have been given to you and the lessons you have learned along the way. Seek the support of positive individuals and surround yourself with people who encourage and inspire you.

Facing Failures as Opportunities for Growth and Learning:

Failures are an integral part of the process of realizing our life purpose. Each failure carries a lesson and an opportunity for growth.

Approach failures with a mindset of learning and resilience.

Recognize that failures do not define your identity or your worth as an individual. See failures as moments of growth, where you can learn what didn't work and make the necessary changes for improvement. Take responsibility for your actions without blaming yourself and focus your energy on how you can do better next time.

Remain open to continuous learning. Ask yourself what you can learn from each failure and how you can utilize those lessons to improve yourself and your path towards your life purpose. Share your experiences with others, as social support can offer a different perspective and valuable support during challenging times.

Conclusion:

In this chapter, we have delved into the importance of facing fears, resistance, and obstacles that can limit our path towards achieving our life purpose. We have discussed strategies for managing self-sabotage and negativity, focusing on self-compassion, self-esteem, and positive thinking. We have also explored how to approach failures as opportunities for growth and learning, maintaining a mindset of resilience and continuous learning. By continuing to overcome these obstacles with determination and commitment, we will be able to progress towards a life of meaning and fulfillment.

Chapter 5:

Creating an Action Plan

Defining Clear and Measurable Goals in Line with Your Life Purpose:

To fulfill your life purpose, it is essential to define clear and measurable goals that align with your vision. Setting specific goals helps you focus your energy and resources in a targeted manner. Here are some suggestions for further exploring this process:

1. Identify long-term goals: Begin by identifying long-term goals that are in line with your life purpose. These goals should represent the general direction you want to take in your life. For example, if your life purpose is to promote education in disadvantaged communities, a long-term goal could be to establish a school in one of these communities.

2. Break down goals into intermediate objectives: Once you have identified

long-term goals, break them down into intermediate objectives. These intermediate objectives represent the necessary steps to achieve the long-term goals. For example, if your long-term goal is to establish a school, an intermediate objective could be to raise funds for its realization.

3. Set short-term goals: Short-term goals are the specific steps you need to take to achieve the intermediate objectives. Ensure that these goals are clear, measurable, and achievable within a defined timeframe. For example, a short-term goal could be to organize a fundraising campaign to collect a certain amount within three months.

Developing an Action Plan to Achieve Your Purpose Step by Step:

Once the goals are defined, it is important to develop a detailed action plan that guides you in achieving those goals. Here are some suggestions for delving into this process:

1. Identify necessary actions: For each goal, identify the specific actions you

need to take to achieve it. Break down each goal into smaller, manageable steps. For example, if your goal is to organize a fundraising campaign, actions could include researching sponsors, planning events, and promoting the campaign.

2. Assign a deadline to each action: Assign a deadline to each action to keep it trackable and hold yourself accountable. This helps maintain a sense of urgency and prevents procrastination. Ensure that the deadlines are realistic and achievable.

3. Organize actions in a logical order: Organize the actions in a logical order that helps you progress consistently towards achieving your goals. Identify dependencies between actions and organize them accordingly. For example, you may want to complete sponsor research before starting to promote the fundraising campaign.

4. Monitor and evaluate your progress: Regularly monitor and evaluate your

progress in achieving the goals. Keep track of what you have accomplished and make any necessary adjustments to your action plan. This periodic evaluation helps you stay focused and make necessary improvements.

Maintaining Motivation and Commitment Along the Journey:

Maintaining motivation and commitment in pursuing your life purpose can be challenging, but there are several strategies you can adopt to stay focused and motivated:

1. Recognize the importance of your purpose: Constantly remind yourself of the importance of your purpose and how achieving the goals contributes to its realization. Keep your passion and enthusiasm for your purpose alive.

2. Review your goals and action plan: Regularly review your goals and action plan to remind yourself of what needs to be done and maintain clarity on your direction. Do this regularly to renew your commitment.

3. Seek inspiration: Seek inspiration from external sources such as books, articles, motivational speeches, or success stories. Exposing yourself to positive experiences can reignite your motivation and make you feel supported on your journey.

4. Find a support system: Seek support from people who share your goals or can provide support and encouragement along the way. A support system helps you overcome challenges and stay focused.

5. Celebrate successes: Celebrate the successes you have achieved along the way, even the small ones. Recognizing your progress gives you a boost of motivation and reminds you that you are making strides toward your purpose.

Conclusion:

In this chapter, we have delved into the importance of creating a detailed action plan to fulfill your life purpose. We have discussed the significance of defining clear and measurable goals in line with your purpose and developing an action plan that guides you step by step toward achieving those goals. Additionally, we have explored various strategies to maintain motivation and commitment along the journey. By continuing to follow your action plan and adopting these strategies, you will be able to steadily progress toward a life of meaning and fulfillment.

Chapter 6:

Living in Harmony with Your Life Purpose

Integrating your life purpose into all spheres of daily life:

To live in harmony with your life purpose, it is crucial to integrate it into all spheres of your daily life. This means that your purpose should be present and influence your actions, thoughts, and decisions in every aspect of your life. Here are some suggestions to delve deeper into this process:

1. Work and career: Seek opportunities to align your work and career with your life purpose. Evaluate if your current job allows you to express your passion and make a meaningful difference in the world. If needed, explore transitioning to a vocation that is more in line with your purpose.

2. Personal relationships: Reflect on how you can integrate your purpose into your personal relationships. Strive to have meaningful and fulfilling relationships that are based on shared values and mutual growth. Be an

inspiring example to others and encourage them to live in alignment with their purpose.

3. Leisure time and hobbies: Find ways to integrate your purpose into your leisure time and hobbies. Choose activities that bring you joy and fulfillment and allow you to express your passions and purpose. For instance, if your purpose is to promote environmental sustainability, you could dedicate part of your free time to gardening or ecological initiatives in your community.

4. Well-being and personal fulfillment: Consider how your purpose can impact your well-being and personal fulfillment. Focus on developing skills and competencies that enable you to pursue your purpose. Look for ways to integrate self-fulfillment practices such as meditation or physical exercise, which help you maintain the balance and mental clarity needed to live in harmony with your purpose.

Experiencing gratitude, happiness, and fulfillment through connection with your purpose:

Living in harmony with your life purpose can bring a profound sense of gratitude, happiness, and fulfillment. Here's how you can deepen this connection:

1. Practice gratitude: Take time to reflect on what you are grateful for in your life, in relation to your purpose. Focus on the positive aspects and opportunities that your purpose has provided. Maintaining a perspective of gratitude will help you keep the connection with your purpose alive.

2. Cultivate happiness: Seek happiness in the small daily things that are aligned with your purpose. Be mindful of activities, people, or events that bring you joy and happiness. Aim to spend more time in these experiences and cultivate a mindset of gratitude and appreciation for them.

3. Recognize achievements and fulfillment: Take stock of the results

and accomplishments you have achieved so far in pursuing your purpose. Acknowledge the obstacles you have overcome and the challenges you have faced. Celebrate your progress and remember that each step forward brings you closer to realizing your purpose.

Creating a balanced and fulfilling life aligned with your purpose:

Living in harmony with your life purpose also requires balancing different spheres of life and creating a fulfilling life that reflects your values and purpose. Here are some considerations to achieve this balance:

1. Set priorities: Identify your priorities based on your life purpose. Dedicate time and energy to activities and relationships that are most meaningful to you. Set boundaries and learn to say "no" to things that are not aligned with your purpose and may distract you from your vision.

2. Create work-life balance: Ensure you allocate time for both work and

personal life. Find a balance that allows you to pursue your purpose without neglecting your well-being and important relationships in your life.

3. Practice self-care: Take care of yourself physically, mentally, and emotionally. Maintain a healthy lifestyle that supports your overall well-being. Engage in activities that rejuvenate you and help you maintain the energy and motivation required to pursue your purpose.

4. Adapt your path: Be flexible in your journey towards your purpose. Consider changes and new opportunities that arise along the way. Adjust your action plan based on circumstances and new information while always keeping your vision and purpose as a guiding force.

Conclusion:

In this chapter, we have explored the importance of living in harmony with your life purpose. We have delved into integrating your purpose into all spheres of daily life, experiencing gratitude, happiness, and fulfillment through connection with your purpose, and creating a balanced and fulfilling life aligned with your purpose. By continuing to cultivate this connection and pursuing a life in alignment with your purpose, you will experience a profound sense of fulfillment and make a significant contribution to your own well-being and that of others.

Final Conclusion:

In this book, we have explored the journey from searching to realizing our life purpose. We have discovered the importance of having a life purpose and the benefits that come from fully embracing it. Through the various chapters, we have addressed different themes that have guided us towards understanding and integrating our purpose into our daily lives.

In the first chapter, we emphasized the significance of having a life purpose and how it can positively impact our well-being and satisfaction. We began our journey of self-exploration in the second chapter, recognizing our unique passions, values, and talents. This helped us develop greater self-awareness and explore the meaningful life experiences that have shaped our identity.

In the third chapter, we utilized practical tools to identify our life purpose, exploring the different spheres of life and strengthening the connection between our personal passions and the impact we wish to have on the world.

In the fourth chapter, we tackled the obstacles that may arise along the way, such as fears, resistances, self-sabotage, and failures. We learned how to manage these challenges and transform them into opportunities for growth and learning.

In the fifth chapter, we created an action plan to translate our purpose into clear and measurable goals, developing strategies to maintain motivation and commitment in pursuing our purpose. Lastly, in the sixth chapter, we explored how to live in harmony with our purpose by integrating it into all aspects of our daily lives, experiencing gratitude, happiness, and fulfillment.

In conclusion, the journey towards discovering and realizing our life purpose is a personal and meaningful one. Each chapter of this book has been designed to guide you in your inner quest and provide you with the tools and knowledge necessary to live in harmony with your purpose. Whether you are just beginning your journey or already making significant progress, remember that the key is to continue to commit, adapt, and grow along the way.

I hope that the information and reflections in this book have inspired you and helped you find your life purpose and live a fulfilling life in alignment with it. In conclusion, I encourage you to embrace your life purpose with joy and determination. Remember that you are a unique individual with unique talents and passions, and your purpose is a gift that you can share with the world. May you find inspiration and courage along your path, facing obstacles with resilience and turning failures into opportunities for growth. May your life be a testament to the power of living in harmony with your purpose, bringing gratitude, happiness, and fulfillment to your daily experience.

I wish for you to create a balanced and fulfilling life that aligns with your purpose, and may your journey be filled with adventures, personal growth, and lasting satisfaction. May your purpose guide you towards a meaningful life and may you leave a positive impact on the world.

Good luck, and may you live a life full of success and fulfillment!